Getting
Published

Getting Published

THE ESSENTIAL IRISH GUIDE

carrowmore.ie

First published 2017

Carrowmore Publishing
50 City Quay
Dublin 2
www.carrowmore.ie

@carrowmore101
info@carrowmore.ie

First Edition

For C.S.

British Library Cataloguing in Publication Data.
A catalogue record for this book is available from the British Library.

ISBN: 978-0-9956108-5-9

Typesetting and origination by Carrowmore
Printed by TJ International Ltd.

Contents

Introduction

Over the last decade, advances in technology, and the resulting shift in the way we both buy and read books, have fundamentally reshaped many aspects of the publishing industry. We now order books online. We read ebooks on our Kindles and smartphones. We download audiobooks to play in the car or the gym or the park.

We also buy books in our local bookshop. We buy glossy hardbacks and paperback fiction, and we do so in ever-greater numbers. We read book reviews in the crumpled supplement of the weekend newspaper over coffee, hear about new releases and book launches through social media and listen to author interviews on the radio.

Some things change and some stay very much the same.

When it comes to getting published, there are, as there always have been, two main routes. These are:

1) To successfully pitch your book to a traditional publisher or to an agent who will find you a publisher.
2) To publish it yourself.

For most authors, the first of these options is also their

first choice. When a publisher takes on your work, they will review the concept of the book, advise you on how to develop it and take the book through the various stages of editorial, design, print or ebook publication. Your publisher will then market and sell your book. The author is normally paid on a royalty basis, through which you get a set percentage of what the publisher receives. Depending on what the publisher sees as the potential size and success of the project, they may pay you an advance on those royalties. That's usually the sum that's referred to when you hear about an author getting 'a book deal'.

The second route is to publish yourself. There was a time when the world of self-publishing was a fairly murky one, carrying the taint of 'vanity publishing'. Over the last five years or so, that perception has changed dramatically (perhaps more than any other area of the book trade), particularly with the advent of digital printing, print-on-demand and ebook publishing. Self-publishing is now relatively easy and, at its most basic level, entirely free. An author can, without any cost other than their time, make their work available as an ebook via Amazon Kindle, Kobo and others. Evading the difficulties that self-published authors historically faced when trying to get their printed books into bookshops, these digital editions will now sit alongside every other book that's published. Some authors have had fantastic success in this way. Just as with traditional publishing, however, these successes tend to involve luck and hard work just as much as raw talent.

The aim of this guide is to shine a light on the business of book publishing and the occasionally opaque process of getting published. Publishing is an old industry that has often cultivated an air of mystery. As a result, a lot of new authors can find themselves either overly daunted by or under-prepared for the various stages of the publication process.

Over the course of this book, we will go through the different publishing routes in more detail, paying particular attention to some of the aspects that frequently cause confusion. While we know that some Irish authors publish with UK or international publishers, we have chosen to focus on Irish publishers and resources here. Hopefully we will leave you knowing what to expect, what might be expected of you, and how to most effectively and successfully approach the task of getting published.

Do I Need a Literary Agent?

The short answer to this is: no, but it will help.

The key role of a literary agent is to place an author's book with the right publisher. What makes a publisher the 'right' choice will obviously vary from one author to the next, but it tends to come down to a combination of the royalties or advance offered, the strength of the publisher's reputation, and the rather more intangible question of a good author–publisher relationship. The author will always make the final decision on which publisher to go with, based on the offers that the agent has been able to generate for them.

Of all the publishers in Ireland that we have come across, only two explicitly stipulate that they do not accept unsolicited submissions. One of these is very large, and one is very small. All other publishers are, in theory at least, open to looking at proposals submitted directly from authors.

Part of the value of an agent, however, is that they can dramatically speed up this process. Realistically, books that come to a publisher from an agent are likely to be looked at far more quickly; they will also be looked at in a more hopeful light, as they have already been vetted. Should you be offered a publishing deal, a literary agent will then negotiate the terms of your contract and argue your case if any dispute arises during the publishing process.

In terms of the finances, literary agents are obviously not free. They are usually paid on commission and, while the rates vary, they tend to be between 15% and 20% of the royalties payable to the author. While this cost is not negligible, bear in mind that the agent is likely to have negotiated as high a rate as possible for those same royalties in the course of discussions with the publisher.

While the upside of a commission arrangement like this is that the agent only gets paid when the author gets paid, the downside for prospective authors is that agents are only in a position to take on proposals with a very strong chance of being quickly accepted by a publisher. The net result is that having an agent will almost always work in the author's favour but, paradoxically, it can often be harder to get an agent than to get a publishing contract.

If you do have an agent, they will be able to discuss with you the different stages of the publishing process that are described in this book. Many authors, though, will not have a relationship with an agent at this stage, so over the course of the following chapters we will try to replicate some of the advice they might offer.

Traditional Publishing

Traditional publishing is the name given to the type of publishing in which an author approaches a publisher with a book proposal, or is approached by the publisher with a suggestion of a book they might write. It is known by various names, from 'traditional publishing' to 'trade publishing' or 'risk publishing'. And it is what people tend to think of when they think of publishing at all.

Under the traditional model, the publisher makes the decision on what they publish, and controls and funds the process. At the risk of stating the obvious, this is what most clearly distinguishes it from self-publishing, in which the author makes all the decisions about how a book will be published. In traditional publishing, the publisher acts as a kind of gatekeeper for the reading public or, alternatively, as a form of benign, often wildly uncommercial, cultural venture fund, through which they find and invest in the talent of writers.

It is a fascinating industry and the Irish publishing sector, while small, has created a platform for some wonderful books and for the careers of some of the greatest writers and artists that the world has known. It is also an old industry, surrounded by a certain mystique that few of its members have felt a pressing need to dispel.

Over the following pages, we will give you some insight into how the traditional publishing process works and what to expect along the way.

Pitching to Publishers

The first thing to remember when putting together your book proposal is that different publishers will have different submission requirements. While the main elements tend to remain largely the same, it is important to take account of these specific differences. Academic publishers, for instance, might require you to submit a CV with details of your academic qualifications, or illustrated publishers might want you to send in sample images or a digital portfolio. That said, the elements that almost always form the core of a good proposal are as follows:

- · A cover letter or email
- · A synopsis of your book
- · Sample chapters
- · A biographical note (or 'author bio')

The cover letter

Your cover letter (or, increasingly, your cover email) will generally be your first contact with a prospective publisher. For this reason, take great care with it. If there was ever an email to proofread, this is the one. No publisher will rule you out on the basis of a typo, and publishers' emails contain them all the time, but it definitely won't improve your chances when you are making a pitch based on your writing ability.

The cover letter should be brief, as the substance of your proposal will be in the attachments. It is really just a note to introduce yourself and your book.

It should mention the name of the publisher, and the name of the commissioning editor if you have it. You may be able to find the name of the relevant editor easily through the publisher's website or via a simple Google search. If not, a good tip is to look at the acknowledgements page of a recent book from that publisher, in which the commissioning editor involved will often be mentioned.

Your cover letter should always make it clear that you know something about the other books on a publisher's list and should explain why yours would be a good fit with them. Putting this information together will take more time than drawing up a generic note that can be sent to any publisher, but it is time well spent. If you decide to keep the core of your letter and tailor it for different publishers, make sure you proofread it with particular care. For an editor, there is nothing worse than reading that an author is very pleased to be sending in her book to you, because she is such a great admirer of another publisher's books.

There are some technical details that an editor will always need in order to get a clear sense of the book. These include:

- Whether your book is complete (and if not, the date when it is likely to be finished).

- Your word count (or your projected final word count).
- For non-fiction, whether you are intending to include images/maps/charts and, if so, how many you are considering.
- For children's books, what age range your book is aimed at.

These details allow an editor to make an initial assessment as to whether this book is a novella or a doorstopper of a sci-fi thriller, a small gift book or something aimed at the specialist reader. If your book is unfinished, you may not know exactly how it will end but, if you have reached the stage where you are ready to submit a proposal, having a clear sense of this is likely to be of as much help to you as your editor.

It will usually work in your favour if the book is complete. Even if the ideal time to release the book may be to coincide with a relevant anniversary or event that is still some way in the future, your publisher will never mind having too *much* time.

If your book is still to be completed, be as realistic as possible about the deadline. It is always better to finish early rather than late. Authors do miss their deadlines sometimes and it tends to cause difficulties. Work will probably have been scheduled for designers and printers; advance information may have been given to bookshops and wholesalers. Rescheduling generally damages a book's chances of success, and certainly sets it off on the wrong foot. For this reason, most publishers will have a clause in their contract that allows them to cancel it if your book is not delivered on time. No publisher would ever want to use this, and certainly no editor wants to have that conversation about a book they may have championed, but it does happen. Setting a target date that you know you can reach will, ultimately, serve everyone far better.

There is nothing wrong with the personality of an author coming through in their cover letter. Publishers want to get a sense of who you are. Do, however, restrain the urge to be too whimsical. Publishing is a nice business, but it is still a business, and being professional is important.

The synopsis

The synopsis of your book is vital. You need to try and convey a complete sense of your work, in as much as this is possible in a single page. If your book is non-fiction, you need to describe the manner in which you are approaching your subject and the reason why your conclusions are different from those of other competing books. It will require some research but, again, this is time well spent. If you are approaching an academic publisher, you might want to include some referees or names of people who could review your work.

Every book, including a non-fiction work, needs to tell a story. You need to engage the reader and take them on a journey; this journey is what your synopsis should convey.

For fiction titles, writing the synopsis can be more difficult. Your editor will already have the sample chapters to judge your writing ability, so the synopsis should really focus on the main characters and the plot. You might also describe which writers have influenced you and which other books yours could be compared to.

If you have a sense of who the target market is, you should mention this; the one caveat is that if you talk about the number of potential readers, it is generally wise to stay on the conservative side of optimism. Your book may be of interest to every English-speaking adult, or to the Irish diaspora as a whole, but if they do all ultimately buy a copy it should be a something to marvel over and enjoy, rather than part of the plan.

Sample chapters

Publishers have a range of different approaches as to how many chapters they require; some might even ask for the full manuscript. In general, however, a selection of sample chapters is all that would be requested at this initial stage. You should obviously choose the chapters that are strongest and most representative of the work, but you should always include the first chapter. Readers may judge a book by its cover, but editors will often judge a proposal by the first few paragraphs. If you lose your editor's interest at that point, it is often hard to get it back.

If your book is accepted, the publisher will of course edit and proofread your work, often several times, but this is never something to rely on when you're submitting your proposal. Your sample chapters should be as good as you can possibly get them and should always be thoroughly proofread before submission. They will never be perfect, just as no finished book is really perfect, but if your writing is full of errors, you greatly increase the chance that the editor will move on to the next proposal on their desk. Bear in mind that an editor will often be reviewing several proposals at the same time, and if another author has taken more care than you, your book may easily fall through the cracks.

Sample chapters for non-fiction and fiction will obviously be quite different, but the point remains the same: you should be entirely happy with the material you submit. Don't send it in until you're ready. If you're not happy with it, your editor probably won't be either.

Author bio

Writers are often reticent when talking about themselves, but your author bio is a very important part of your submission and should never be omitted. The publisher needs to know who they might be working with, and you may well have a lot of information to include here that will be of benefit to your proposal.

For instance, you should include any writing experience you have had, whether that is previous books you have written, articles for newspapers or journals, short stories or essays. If you have ever won any prizes or awards for your writing, of course your editor will want to know this.

You may have heard that in 2013, a novel called *The Cuckoo's Calling* was published by Sphere Books, from a debut author, Robert Galbraith. Galbraith did not include in his submission the full extent of his writing experience. Later that year, it emerged that Galbraith was a pen-name, formed by choosing the first name of the author's political hero (Robert F. Kennedy) and the surname of the author's childhood fantasy name (Ella Galbraith). Mr Galbraith did get a publishing deal, which was great, though if the author had revealed that her real name was J.K. Rowling and she had enjoyed a relatively successful career to date, you can imagine that the deal might have been even easier to strike.

Aside from writing experience, it is very useful for publishers to know whether you have any media experience and whether you are happy to do radio or television interviews. The process of publicizing a book can often involve interviews, talks and speaking at panel events, so if this is something you are comfortable with, make sure the publisher is aware of it.

For non-fiction authors who are experts in their fields, it is crucial to give the publisher full details of your experience, describing your career to date and listing any relevant organizations of which you are a member.

While having a strong social media presence is not the holy grail that it is sometimes made out to be, if you do have a significant following for reasons connected with the subject of your book, make sure to include this in your author bio. If not, don't worry about it too much.

Once you have sent in your proposal to the publisher, be prepared to wait a while for an answer. Publishers tend to receive a lot of submissions; they all have to be reviewed with the care that you would want given to your own work. The publisher's website will sometimes give a guide as to the time you should expect to wait for a response but, as a rule of thumb, it may take six to eight weeks. If you haven't heard back within that time, feel free to send a follow-up email or telephone the publisher, but do be as patient and pleasant as you can. Their relationship with the author is very important to editors, and they will be more likely to want to work with someone they like; it's just human nature.

If the first (or second) publisher you contact doesn't offer you a publishing deal, don't be disheartened. Publishers will always turn down far more books than they take on; remember that your book might simply not fit with their list, for any number of reasons. Don't forget the many incredibly successful authors whose books were initially turned down, including William Golding's *Lord of the Flies*, Margaret Mitchell's *Gone with the Wind* and Beatrix Potter's *The Tale of Peter Rabbit*. And, of course, J.K. Rowling.

If, however, you do receive an offer of publication, the next step will be your publishing contract, so we will turn to that in the next chapter.

The Publishing Contract

The secrets of the publishing contract have long been shrouded in mystery. Contracts are traditionally drawn up on a delicate vellum, in a book-lined opium den down a little-known alley near Postman's Park. Once complete, they are rolled tightly and stored in a tall contract-shaped hat. The hat-wearer, as she is universally known, then casually cycles her penny farthing around the great publishing houses of the land, where she is greeted with awe and responds with silence.

From there, the lesser lights of the industry pass the scroll from manicured hand to less-manicured hand until it reaches the trembling palm of a newly appointed editorial assistant. On hearing the knock at her door, she emerges, blinking, from the mass of proposals and spreadsheets that wall her in. She opens the dusty ledger and carefully updates the publishing programme; she rings the bell, releases the dove and, lo, the contract is sent off to the author in the post.

Or…

Each publishing house has a template stored somewhere on their shared computer server; your contract will be based on this. The name and address of the author will change; the title of the book and the delivery date will change. But nothing else is ever likely to change that much.

There are a few points that any good contract should cover and we will list these here, so that you can be sure to check them.

Firstly, it should state clearly who the parties to the contract are (usually you, as the author, and the publisher), as well as the date on which the contract is being made.

It should also state the title of your book. Don't worry if this is a working title only, as the title is one of the elements that often changes at some point during the publication process. The publisher will usually reserve the right to decide on the final title, based on their experience and the feedback they receive from booksellers, but they will always act in the best interests of the book. As a result, they will be able to explain exactly why they are making any changes of this kind.

The contract should specify what rights you are granting to the publisher under this agreement. Most commonly, these are world rights in the English language in all formats, including both print and electronic. The copyright of the work will generally remain with the author; what is being granted to the publisher is a licence to publish the book and also to sell subsidiary rights (like foreign rights or film rights). There may well be room for negotiation about which rights are assigned to the publisher, but the important thing is that everyone is very clear about the end result and understands exactly what the wording in the contract refers to.

The contract should also specify what is required of the author. This will cover issues such as when the book is due to be delivered, what its length will be and whether the author is expected to provide illustrations, an index or any other supplementary elements. It will also ask the author to confirm that the work is entirely their own, does not infringe anyone else's copyright and contains nothing libelous, defamatory or liable in any other way to expose the publisher to legal action. Many contracts will contain an indemnity clause, whereby the author indemnifies the publisher against legal action for any of these issues.

It is important to check that your contract covers the question of 'reversion of rights', as this has become far more important in the age of ebooks and print-on-demand. A reversion of rights clause explains what happens after the book goes out of print, or if the sales fall below a certain level after a certain period of time; alternatively, it may simply set a time-frame for the duration of the contract. The idea is that this will allow the author to recover their rights from the publisher in the event that the book stops selling, usually after a specified number of years. Setting a time-frame for the contract as a whole would be quite unusual in Ireland and the UK, but there should certainly be some kind of clause, usually relating to the book becoming unavailable and the publisher declining to reprint, that will allow the author to recover their rights in the work.

Publishing Ireland, the Irish Book Publishers' Association, has created a Code of Practice adhered to by all their member publishers, which gives more information on many of the points about contracts discussed here. This Code of Practice can be viewed at www.publishingireland.com.

One of the major functions of any publishing contract, of course, is to describe the arrangement regarding advances and royalties. Given their importance, we will cover this issue in more specific detail in the next chapter.

Advances and Royalties

The advance

The advance. That elusive, bejewelled dancing elephant at the end of the negotiating table. When you hear on the news or in the trade press about a deal being struck with a first-time author, the figure that is mentioned will always be the advance. If it's in the news, it's probably significant, and for some authors it is the thought of these often life-changing amounts of money that keeps them driven in the small hours.

But what exactly are advances? Why are they paid? And how is the amount decided on?

To start at the beginning, the advance is an advance payment of the royalties that will be earned by the author. It is not an additional payment; once the advance has been paid, the author will receive no royalties until this sum has been earned out.

In the event that sales of the book are not high enough for the advance payment to earn out, nothing happens – at least to the author. It is generally accepted that this is the publisher's risk and they won't usually try to get the money back.

There are some limited circumstances in which an advance may need to be repaid by the author; these circumstances would be specified in your contract, but the most common one is non-delivery of the finished work. If you don't deliver the book, or go so far beyond your deadline that it no longer makes sense for the publisher to release the book, it would be fairly standard to have a legally binding facility for the advance to be repaid.

To limit the publisher's exposure, advances are often split into three parts: one third becomes payable on signature of contract; one third becomes payable on delivery of the final manuscript; and the final payment is made on publication of the work. It is quite normal for a contract to be structured in this fashion.

The question of how much the advance should be is intrinsically linked to the question of why an advance is paid at all, so this is what we will look at first.

Why is an advance on royalties ever paid? The answer to this depends largely on your perspective, and each answer provides a useful, if partial, explanation of the process.

One of the reasons you often hear is that payment of an advance can allow an author the time and space to finish a work, free from financial constraint. On a related note, there may be expenses involved in the author's research that can be mitigated by the advance. There is an element of truth in this, particularly for very large advances. For instance, if we're talking about a very high-profile non-fiction author with a strong publishing track record, whose work will involve significant travel or in-depth investigation, the advance could be critical to the completion of the book. This, however, is relatively rare and not a complete explanation in itself because it so rarely applies.

From a second perspective, the payment of an advance can be construed to show a commitment on behalf of the publisher to the author. Skin in the game, and so forth. This is an argument often made to try and influence the payment of an advance, rather than being a truly convincing reason in itself. The publisher will, in fact, already be showing a significant commitment to the author by taking on their work and investing in it, through providing editorial, design and marketing support. So, while this argument may be used by all parties (possibly including your editor) to justify the decision to pay an advance, it doesn't fully explain why the payment is made.

The third perspective, and possibly the most compelling, is one of simple market forces. If an author is choosing between a number of publishers, all offering the same royalty rate and the same level of editorial quality, it may well be the size of the advance that makes up their mind. It isn't always entirely straightforward, however. If, as an author, you are presented with a choice between a publisher offering a low royalty but a high advance, a publisher offering a medium-level advance but whose list doesn't seem to be a perfect fit with your book, and a third option in which a publisher offers no advance and a low royalty but their books are amazing and sell well, what do you do? This may depend on how much you value the cash in hand, and there is no right or wrong answer.

Most publishers put together a financial forecast for a book based on the first print run, which might be enough stock to last 6 or 12 or 18 months. They look at what the costs will be, particularly editorial, design, marketing and print. They look at the net revenue that the sales of that print run will generate (net revenue being the amount the publisher receives after granting standard discounts to bookshops or online retailers). Once these figures are worked out, they will have a relatively clear idea of how much the author is due to earn in royalties if the first print run sells out completely. In offering an advance, they take this amount as the upper limit. Exactly how much of it they choose to offer as an advance will depend on the factors mentioned above, together with how much risk they are prepared to take on, and what the business model of the publisher is.

After all, nobody can ever be 100% sure that a book will sell 100% of its print run. If they were, it would be a very easy business. And if a publisher is taking a chance on a new author, for example, they would be unlikely to couple that risk with the risk of an advance of any substantial size.

It's worth remembering that the advance is only one factor to bear in mind in publishing your book. Some of the most important and valuable books being written today have earned no advance at all, and in the case of specialist academic works which have a very small market but can be of fundamental importance in their field, the author's university may even have paid a subsidy to the publisher. For every author who has been offered a major advance there are hundreds who have had none at all, and it can just as easily be a book from this second pool that ends up changing the world.

Royalties

At the heart of the financial relationship between an author and a publisher is the question of royalties. The level of royalties may be different from publisher to publisher and from book to book, but it is important to understand how they work, how and when they are paid and how this is laid out in your contract.

First of all, there are two types of royalties: 'gross royalties' and 'net royalties'. Gross royalties are based on a percentage of the cover price of the book. Net royalties are based on a percentage of what the publisher receives for every book sold. For instance, if a book is a hardback, priced at €20, and the author's contract specifies a gross royalty of 5%, the author will receive €1 for each copy sold. If the author's contract for the same book specifies a net royalty of 10%, and the publisher sells a copy to a large bookshop at a 50% discount, the author will, again, receive €1 on this particular sale.

In Ireland and the UK, net royalties are now more common than gross royalties, so this is likely to be the system you find described in your contract. Both have their advantages, so the main thing is just to be clear on what kind of royalty you are receiving.

Royalty rates can vary widely. Authors of some academic titles, for instance, will receive no royalties at all on the first print run. The reason for this is that these highly specialist books often make either a very small amount of profit or none at all. For most academic authors, their reasons for publishing are not wholly commercial, so this tends not to cause a problem as long as there is some way for them to benefit in the event that the book becomes a surprise hit.

For more commercial publishers, royalty rates can vary from 5% net up to (in a small number of cases) 20% net. The average in Ireland appears to be in the region of 10%.

In recent years there has been quite a lot of public debate about the amount that authors earn, so this may be a good time to look in more detail at how publishers decide what they can offer in the way of royalties.

As an example, let's take a hardback book in a 'royal' format (which is the large hardback format you will commonly see used for new non-fiction titles). The recommended retail price is €20 and the book is 300 pages long. The print run for this book is 1,000 copies and the royalty rate for the author is 10% net.

The publisher sells the book to a large high-street bookshop chain, at a discount of 50%. This means that the publisher will receive €10. The author will then receive €1.

On the face of it, this seems like a stark disparity, but it's worth looking a little further. The argument from the publisher's perspective goes something like this: from the €10 the publisher has received, they have now paid €1 to the author, leaving €9. From that €9, they will pay the printer; for a book in this format being printed in these numbers, the cost is likely to be roughly €2 per book, leaving the publisher with €7. From that €7, they will pay for physical distribution and sales representation, which will cost approximately €2, leaving €5. From that €5, the publisher will also pay for the editing, design, cover design, proofreading, publicity and marketing of the book, alongside their accounting and the basic overheads for the business.

As a result, it is quite likely that an Irish publisher will earn the same amount of money per book as the author, at least on the first edition.

You will sometimes hear unflattering comparisons made between the royalties paid by traditional publishers and the royalties paid by Amazon's Kindle Direct programme, under which an author can earn up to 70%, rather than 10%. Bear in mind, though, that under this model Amazon doesn't pay for editorial, design or marketing; it is important to compare like with like.

Ebook royalties tend to be higher than print royalties; at the moment, the standard ebook royalty in Ireland and the UK seems to lie between 20% and 25%. The rate is higher because the print costs are no longer a factor. But it is not, obviously, at the same rate as the Amazon Kindle royalties, because other costs aside from print still remain, such as those relating to editorial, design and marketing.

Of course, if a book takes off and goes into many more editions and print runs, both the author and publisher can start to benefit financially.

When you look at the royalty clause in your contract, check that the percentage is clearly stated and that the contract specifies whether the royalties are gross or net.

Royalties are paid at least once a year, but more commonly twice, so that you receive payment for six-month blocks of sales. Whenever you receive a royalty statement, it should be accompanied by a statement of sales. This will list how many copies of the book have been sold in each format, whether that's hardback, paperback or ebook. Your contract should always state when your royalties will be paid each year.

Once you have signed a contract for publishing your book, it is important to keep a copy. In the vast majority of cases, there are no problems between authors and publishers; the author–publisher relationship is often long and extremely positive. However, it is useful to have a reference point that you can return to, if you do need to discuss any issues with your publisher further down the line. Good fences, after all, make good neighbours.

Editorial and Design

Once you have delivered your finished manuscript to the publisher, the next stage is the copyediting of the book. This may happen in-house, or the publisher may outsource the work to a specialist freelance editor. The use of freelance editors has become much more common in recent years; most publishers will outsource at least some elements of their editorial work.

At this stage, the manuscript is still in the format of a Word document. The copyeditor will look at issues such as clarity of language and meaning, spelling and grammar, dates and references. A publisher will usually have a house style and the copyeditor will make changes to ensure that the book conforms to that style.

A good copyeditor will not re-write your book in their own voice, but will rather look to bring out the best in your writing. There are many highly talented editors working in Ireland and the UK and the experience they bring to your book is greatly to be valued. The relationship between author and editor is one that requires a substantial degree of trust; in the majority of cases that trust is amply rewarded.

When the editorial stage is complete, the publisher will arrange the internal design. This is the process in which the book is laid out by a designer within the chosen format, in order to create the page proofs. The complexity of this will vary hugely from genre to genre. For text-only books, like novels or business books, the design can be relatively simple and fast. For illustrated titles, like cookbooks or some children's books, it can be a very elaborate process; the publisher and author may, in some cases, be working with illustrators, photographers or graphic designers, in addition to the publisher's in-house team.

Once the page proofs are complete, they will usually be proofread by the publishers in the first instance. Authors often ask what the difference is between copyediting and proofreading: while there are some variations in the definition of these processes, the general understanding is that copyediting involves working with the text in its original form, usually from a Word document, whereas proofreading involves working with the designed proofs. This means that proofreaders have an opportunity to catch any errors that have slipped through the copyediting process, but are also responsible for identifying problems that may have arisen during the design stage.

After the proofs have been corrected by the publisher, they are sent to the author for a second check. The author knows the book intimately, and there are always some issues that will be noticed by the author more readily than by anybody else, so this is a crucial stage of the editorial process and should never be missed. Having said that, the proofreading stage is not the time for substantial parts of the book to be re-written. There will always be a temptation to start re-wording sentences that suddenly strike you as unsatisfactory, but your publisher will thank you for only doing this when absolutely necessary.

The cover design will usually take place at the same time as the editing and internal design stages, as a publisher's marketing and sales team need the front cover to be available as far in advance as possible. The cover will be required for the publisher's catalogue and also for the sales representatives to present the book to bookshops, which can happen several months ahead of publication.

The cover design can be an emotive issue for the author, so it is worth examining in more detail how publishers handle this. Everyone is happiest when the author and publisher agree on what the cover should look like, and the design of the cover is usually a collaborative process, but the publisher will tend to have the final say. The front cover is one of the most important sales and marketing tools available; the publisher, by virtue of their experience of the industry and the skill of the designer they employ, should be best placed to know what kind of cover will work to the book's advantage. As with the copyediting stage, this requires a degree of trust on the author's part. We recommend having faith in your publisher and remembering why you chose to work with them in the first place.

Briefly, the process works like this: the editor, in consultation with the author and the sales and marketing team, puts together a cover brief for the designer. This brief will specify the title, subtitle, author name and back cover text; it may also include examples of cover styles that the editor likes (or indeed doesn't like), along with any artwork or photographs that may be included. This should ideally give the cover designer parameters within which they can work, without being so prescriptive as to limit the value of the designer's experience.

Seeing the final version of a book cover should be quite a special moment for you as an author, possibly only topped by seeing your book on the shelves of a bookshop for the first time. In a long and involved journey, it is a moment to savour.

Once the cover and internals of a book have been checked, re-checked and signed off, it's time for the publisher to send your book to press …

Sales and Marketing

The moment you secure a publishing deal, the hard work ends and the hard work begins. The moment you type the last words of your manuscript, the hard work ends and the hard work begins. And the moment the finished copies of your freshly minted book arrive on your doorstep, the hard work ends and, once again, the hard work begins.

Although different publishers have different resources at their disposal, the steps that follow the publication of a book tend to be very similar. Copies will have been sold in advance to the wholesalers and the larger bookshops. The two principal wholesalers in Ireland are Eason and Argosy, both of which will buy copies and sell them on to smaller bookshops. Larger bookshops, such as Hodges Figgis and the Waterstones bookshops, Dubray, O'Mahony's in Limerick, Kenny's in Galway and Liam Russell's in Cork, will usually order directly from the publisher. In the days following its release, your book will (hopefully!) start to appear in some or all of these, as well as the many excellent smaller and independent bookshops across the country.

How do the various booksellers know about your book? The answer is that the sales team at your publisher have 'pitched' the book to them months in advance. They have shown them the cover, talked about the retail price, discussed discounts and presented the marketing and publicity plans. Based on these conversations, each bookshop places their order.

Authors sometimes ask if a publisher can 'get a book into' a particular bookshop; it's important to remember that the shop is actually *buying* the book at this point, so the final decision has to be up to them. The discounts that are given to booksellers range from 35% to 55% of the retail price, depending on the volume of books that are ordered by (or have historically been ordered by) the shop.

One of the quirks about the Irish and UK book trade is that books are sold to shops on a sale-or-return basis. This means that a shop buys a certain number of books and, if all goes well, they sell out and order more copies. If the book doesn't sell as well as expected, the shop can, after a time, return these books to the publisher. This is an aspect of the book trade that is hotly debated by publishers at regular intervals, but there are no signs of anything changing soon. The current model presents both pros and cons for publishers and authors. The cons are probably obvious: the publisher will never know exactly how many copies are 'fully' sold at any point. A thousand copies of a book might have been sold to bookshops in the spring, but hundreds of these might come back to the publisher in the autumn. There are good points about the system too, though, as it allows bookshops to take a chance on new and emerging writers or on smaller publishers, and give them shelf space and an opportunity to sell. If the model was changed to what is known as 'firm sale', there would be greater certainty all round, but also very likely a far smaller range of books available in the shops. It is worth knowing how the system works at the moment, if for no other reason than allowing you to avoid ever wishing an author 'many happy returns' on their birthday.

An essential part of the process at this point is making the public as fully aware of the new book as possible. Review copies will be sent to the national print media and to trade publications like *Books Ireland*; author interviews may be arranged for radio programmes such as The Book Show, Talking Books, Sean O'Rourke, Pat Kenny or Sean Moncrieff, alongside the broad array of excellent local radio stations around the country. Radio in Ireland has traditionally been a great supporter of books and writers, and radio interviews are an exceptionally good way to spread the word about your book.

Just as with selling to bookshops, getting press or radio coverage is also competitive. The newspaper space dedicated to books is enormously important but limited; in any one week there will be far more books submitted to a newspaper than there are book pages. Likewise, the radio stations are always looking for good content and interesting interviews, but there are plenty of appealing books and ideas being pitched to them every week, so wide coverage for your book can never be guaranteed. It is, however, fairly likely to be covered in some form, and the press in Ireland is regarded as being genuinely supportive of local authors and Irish-published books.

Your publisher may also arrange to have their authors involved in the various literary events, panels and festivals that take place throughout the country. There are a wide range of these, including the Listowel International Writers Festival, the West Cork Literary Festival and the Dublin Book Festival.

There are many ways to try to publicize a book; we have only listed the most obvious strategies here. The most important thing to remember is that the more closely an author is involved in the efforts to promote their book, the better the book always seems to do.

And, of course, there is always the book launch!

In general, though, we find it is best to view the launch less as a publicity event than an opportunity for the author and their friends and family to celebrate this great achievement. Members of the media do get invited to launches, but they are invited to so many each week that they should never really be the focus. Invite the people you will be happy to see in the crowd when you look around the room.

We have attended book launches in all kinds of places, from bookshops and libraries to the ballroom of the Shelbourne Hotel and the deck of an Irish naval vessel. Most venues are very happy to host a launch, and your publisher will always be on hand to help.

In preparation for your own launch, you might consider attending a launch of somebody else's book to see how they work. In the next chapter, the last in this section, we will offer our thoughts on how best to approach being a guest at another author's book launch.

How to Survive a Book Launch

First things first, never arrive on time. If the launch is at 7pm, don't dream of being there before midnight. If you do, you will likely be the first, and will immediately be introduced to the author and all his family. He will shake your hand with a confused half-smile as his wife debates whether you are a relative, colleague or lover. Perhaps all three. She will press a glass of warm white wine into your hand and surreptitiously give you a sniff. There have been times, she remembers, when there have been fading trails of perfume on her husband's jacket. Too subtle to arouse suspicion, just real enough to spark a pleasant fantasy. Of course he was just standing beside someone on the bus, but what if, what if, what if? This, however, is different. Why else would this person be here at this time? She will look at you and inhale so deeply that your wispy scarf will immediately fly up her nose, sending all three of your glasses tumbling gracefully skyward. The muffled, snuffled roar of her surprise will be all the more poignant as a gentle rain of Chardonnay falls upon the collective brow. All that will be left is for you to mop the hair from your visage, shake the author's dampened hand once more, and wish him every success. Again.

Assuming you have the good sense to avoid this trap, you will be arriving at the perfect moment, a decent crowd having filled the room and taken away the desolate fear that looms over every book launch that's ever been, ever. The speeches will be moments away, leaving you just enough time to settle in.

Your entrance is always something to take seriously. You may think you know somebody there, but when you arrive you are more likely to see Halley's Comet playing dice in a corner with the devil. You will know nobody, and it's important to prepare for that. Do not walk through the room, scanning the crowd, smiling ever more anxiously, like one of those passengers who comes through the arrival gates of the airport, looking around for friends and family with banners and hugs and flowers, and ends up walking steadily more slowly, face dropping with every step, before wrapping their coat more tightly about them, blinking back the tears and wheeling themselves out into the rain. Don't ever be that person.

Keep your head down, and make your way to wherever the books are being sold. Don't ever think it's ok to avoid buying a book at a launch. Yes, they will notice; yes, it looks cheap; no, they're not too busy to see. Just buy the book.

It will also give you something to do for that first crucial minute. Stride through the crowd like a proud and happy lion, directly to the tiny table. Pay with cash, and ideally have exact change. This is a book table. That person is probably an editorial assistant, living on breadcrumbs and sugar. Wall Street is far away from this table. If you feel an urge to suck your teeth and arch a brow when you hear the price of the book, restrain it. It's fine.

Once you have your book, you can safely swoop by the drinks table and, making doubly sure they see your purchase, partake, partake. It will strengthen you for the next leg of the adventure.

The speeches will generally begin with an editor, bookseller, or friend of the still-damp author tapping gingerly on the microphone. You will be relieved to learn that all of the ladies and all of the gentlemen remain very welcome.

And then we're off. Keep an eye on the crowd for people you think may be thanked. Place a bet with yourself. Win. When someone is thanked, give yourself double points if they smile deprecatingly, bow their heads and give a slight nod. If someone accepts their praise by pulling their t-shirt over their head, sprinting around the podium and sliding across the carpet, you are at the best launch ever.

As you will be clutching your wine, clapping should be done by hand to forearm. Stick with the same forearm throughout to avoid any confusion with the Haka.

When the speeches finish, drain your wine and leave. Never hang around. Do, however, make sure to wink at the author as you go. And, of course, his wife.

'How to Survive a Book Launch' was first published in 2015 as the winner of The Listowel International Writers' Festival Originals Category.

Self-Publishing

Even more so than traditional publishing, self-publishing has changed out of all recognition over the last twenty years. The advent of print-on-demand technology, coupled with the rise of the ebook, transformed it from what was once the province of the vain and the brave to a thriving sector of the publishing landscape and led to an explosion in the amount of writing being published. New digital platforms have also allowed for this process to be, at its simplest level, entirely free, with no costs at all to the author.

There is more than one caveat to that last statement, however, as many authors and readers have discovered. When an author publishes with a reputable traditional publisher, their book will be edited, professionally designed, proofread, printed, marketed, distributed and sold. When an author steps over that dividing line and becomes a publisher themselves, the reasons for those steps do not cease to exist. An author may be able to take a book through all of these stages single-handedly, wearing hats of many colours, or they may use the services of freelancers or publishing companies, but these steps really do still need to happen. The most successful self-published authors would readily testify to this.

Stephen Page, in his address to the Publishing Ireland Trade Day in 2014, squarely addressed the divisions that have long existed between traditional publishers and self-publishing authors. Page was the CEO of Faber & Faber, one of the oldest and most revered of traditional publishing houses, with more right than most to be sniffy. In contrast, however, he said that he felt self-publishers were prime examples of the 'atomic publisher', colleagues rather than rivals, and fully deserving of our respect. For Page, the new divide was not between self-publishing and traditional publishing, but only between good and bad publishing.

We could not agree with this more.

The Steps of Self-Publishing

As we have mentioned previously, the steps a self-published book goes through are, ideally, very similar to those of traditional publishing.

Of course, a traditional publisher will usually have a greater number of people involved in the process. There may be acquisitions meetings, cover meetings, marketing meetings and sales conferences. The self-publishing process is far more streamlined, but the essential steps will still be the same, and these are as follows:

- Copyediting
- Design
- Cover design
- Proofreading
- Printing and/or ebook conversion
- Sales and marketing

There will be nuances and variations to this process for every book, of course, but if these key elements are covered, a self-published author should not be at any significant disadvantage. We will now look briefly at the key questions that may arise for self-publishing authors at each stage of the process.

Copyediting

If an author is asking a reader to spend their time and money on a book, there are few things more damaging than seeing a host of errors in the first few pages. Even when an author has real talent, poor editing may mean that it is never discovered or appreciated.

Most writers who get to the point of completing an entire book can write well. They may have been asked to edit or proofread the work of other writers. It is almost impossible, though, to properly edit your own writing, as you tend to read what you think should be on the page rather than what's actually there.

We once had the great honour of copyediting a piece by Seamus Heaney, a foreword for a very important book. At this stage, Heaney had already been awarded the Nobel Prize for Literature, so the prospect was daunting. However, we did find things to correct, and he agreed that they should be changed. At that stage in our career, this was the editorial equivalent of being shot into space, but it brought home the reality that no author can ever properly edit their own work. Books really do need editors.

Design

When an author is self-publishing for the first time, they are sometimes a little unclear about the importance of what happens between the end of the writing and editing process and the start of the printing. A book will normally be written as an A4 Word document. This allows it to be printed on standard office printers and is perfect for most things. But if you look on the shelves of any bookshop, you will see that very few books are A4. They are royal octavo or Trade B; they are bespoke landscape editions or small pocket guides. The choices are endless, but they are very rarely A4. Historically, the reasons for this are economic ones, as books in formats like royal octavo (234 x 156mm) were more efficient for printers to produce, which made them cheaper. Over time, the fact that publishers were printing in these formats made them into the formats that 'books looked like'.

Obviously there are nuances and exceptions to this, but it is crucial to factor in a design stage for every book, in order to take it from its A4 Word document format into a size and layout that is ready for printing. This can be a relatively simple process or an exceptionally involved one, depending on the book. In every case, though, a good designer will add significant value to your book, through a host of tiny elements that you might not even see at first, from adding running heads and addressing 'widows' and 'orphans' to providing guidance on font choice, margin width and chapter head pages. To drop a cap or not to drop a cap? Indeed.

Cover design

There is no need to labour the point about the importance of good cover design for increasing the readership of your book. If you can stretch to having your cover professionally designed, it really is money well spent.

The cost of cover design can vary significantly, depending on the skill and experience of the designer. There are some exceptionally good designers out there, and many who work solely on freelance projects, so there are plenty of skilled people available if your budget allows.

If you decide to design the cover yourself, bear in mind that, just as with the internals of your book, the printer will want a cover of the correct dimensions, with the correct spine width, and in the appropriate format for printing, which is almost always as a PDF.

Once you're comfortable that all the technical aspects have been satisfactorily dealt with, you can turn to considering the more aesthetic elements: the choice of font, colour and imagery, the tone of the blurb, the layout of the title, sub-title and author name. If we were to offer three simple tips to authors designing their own covers for the first time, they would be as follows:

1. The best repository of sample covers in the world is Amazon. Browse to see what you like.
2. Don't try to get across every element of the book in the cover. The reader won't thank you for it. Focus on tone.
3. Never say 'By' before the author's name on the cover. Just write the name.

Proofreading

As proofreading, unlike copyediting, takes place after the design stage, this is an opportunity not only to check the 'content' of the book but to look at aspects associated with the design and layout. For instance, if your book has running heads, make sure these are all correct; check that the page numbers in the Table of Contents are accurate, as the pagination of the book may have changed several times over the course of the design; look for missing full stops at the end of paragraphs (for some reason, this is something that always seems to crop up). These are just a few examples; the main point of the proofreading stage is to act as one final sweep, picking up on any small errors that have slipped through the copyedit or may even have been introduced during the design process.

Printing / ebook conversion

If you are working with a publishing services company, they will probably arrange the print stage and ebook conversion for you. If you are arranging the printing yourself, we would offer the following tips:

1. There are no set prices for book printing, as the cost for each book is different depending on its format, page extent, binding and print run.
2. The more you print, the lower the cost per book becomes. The skill is in not overprinting or underprinting, so try to gauge the realistic size of the market and balance this with how much you have to spend.
3. Get more than one quote.

It is also worth factoring in the value of print-on-demand (POD) technology. There are now platforms that will allow your book to be printed as and when copies are bought, reducing the need to store large numbers of copies or, indeed, any copies at all. Having copies available purely via POD means that online readers can easily buy your book but, realistically, it will probably not be stocked in the bookshops. For that reason, a lot of Irish authors take a dual approach, printing a set quantity for the bookshops and having an edition available online via POD.

If your book is to be an ebook, there are a number of companies who can help you with the conversion of your work into an ebook format, or you can even potentially do this yourself with a little time and practice.

Sales and marketing

The best advice we could give to a self-publishing author who is at the point of starting their sales and marketing campaign is to replicate, as far as possible, the way in which a traditional publisher deals with the booktrade. There may well be additional elements that a self-publishing author can bring to the task, but if you are approaching bookshops, we would always advocate doing this in the way in which bookshops are used to being approached. By this, we mean that you should put together a one-page document that contains all the details of your book, including the bibliographic information, the price and the ISBN. Include your front cover and any relevant publicity details. Also, you need to know what discount you will be able to offer the bookshop, as they will definitely ask.

The same is true for the radio stations and the press. Use what contacts you can, give them all the information they need, and be as patient as it is ever possible to be when you have a new book out and are very understandably waiting for the phone to ring.

If you have decided that the bulk of your marketing efforts will be online, there are a wealth of options, including social media advertising, blogging and setting up your own website. Quite a lot of online marketing can be carried out without cost, so balance this with the size of your budget and the return that you are hoping for.

A Manifesto for Self-Publishers

In 2015, *The Bookseller* launched its 'Five Minute Manifesto' series, in which people working in various areas of the publishing industry set out their principles, rules and hopes for the future of the book business. There were manifestos on reading and readers, on digital formats and on what a new business model for publishing might look like.

As part of this, we were delighted to agree to write the manifesto for self-publishing companies. We are very happy to reproduce that original 'manifesto' here.

Be more than a printer

There is more to being a publisher than being a printer, and there is more to being a self-publishing company than offering to print books. Authors should be able to avail themselves of copyediting, proofreading and proper cover design. If you can't offer these to your author, you can still advise your authors of their importance and point them in the right direction.

Be transparent

Authors who use the services of a self-publishing company should know how much everything will cost before work begins, and this cost should be final. This should apply to copyediting and to cover design as well as every other service offered. There should be no hidden costs or vagaries.

Be knowledgeable

If an author comes to you with a query about a particular genre, be it children's publishing, YA fiction or graphic novels, know what the print or marketing trends are, or any other elements that it's important for them to know. If you don't know, research it. Your author is paying for your industry knowledge as well.

Be honest

Not every book will be a bestseller, and not every book is written with that as its goal. But be honest about the success stories of other self-published authors, and acknowledge that while it might be easier than in the past to reach readers, it can still be hard and may not always work.

When an ISBN is registered, it appears on thousands of databases online. Authors should know that this is an automatic data feed, and does not mean their book has been stocked in all of these places.

Be respectful

Traditional publishers provide support for their authors in all sorts of ways, from encouragement to wise counsel when they can offer it.

There is no reason that a self-publishing author should not receive that same level of support and respect just because they are choosing to pay for your time.

This 'manifesto' was first published in The Bookseller *in 2015 as part of Porter Anderson's Futurebook series.*

The Traditional Publishers

Appletree Press

www.appletree.ie

_____

A member of Publishing Ireland,
the Irish Book Publishers' Association

_____

What do they publish?

General non-fiction
Fiction
Sport
Guidebooks

Contact details:

Post: 164 Malone Road, Belfast BT9 5LL
Email: reception@appletree.ie
Tel: 0044 (0) 28 90 24 30 74
Twitter: @AppletreePress

Editorial note:

Publish in eight languages. Chris Murphy is a board
member of Publishing Ireland.

Artisan House Editions

www.artisanhouse.ie

A member of Publishing Ireland,
the Irish Book Publishers' Association

What do they publish?

Lifestyle
Food
Art & music
Poetry

Contact details:

Post: Letterfrack, Connemara, Co. Galway
Email: artisanhouseeditions@gmail.com
Tel: 00 353 (0) 91 452031
Twitter: @ArtisanH

Editorial note:

Founded in 2013. Recent publications include *An Art Lover's Guide to the French Riviera*.

Ashfield Press

www.ashfieldpress.ie

What do they publish?

General non-fiction
Biography
Cookery

Contact details:

Post: 30 Linden Grove, Blackrock, Co Dublin
Email: info@ashfieldpress.com
Tel: 00 353 (0)1 288 9808
Twitter: n/a

Editorial note:

Limited number of traditional publishing proposals being
considered currently. Also run Linden Press.

Atrium Press

www.corkuniversitypress.com

———————

A member of Publishing Ireland,
the Irish Book Publishers' Association

———————

What do they publish?

Lifestyle
Cookery
Photography

Contact details:

Post: Youngline Industrial Estate,
Pouladuff Road, Cork
Email: corkuniversitypress@ucc.ie
Tel: 00 353 (0) 21 490 2980
Twitter: @CorkUP

Editorial note:

An imprint of Cork University Press.

Attic Press

www.corkuniversitypress.com

A member of Publishing Ireland,
the Irish Book Publishers' Association

What do they publish?

Women's studies

Contact details:

Post: Youngline Industrial Estate,
Pouladuff Road, Cork
Email: corkuniversitypress@ucc.ie
Tel: 00 353 (0) 21 490 2980
Twitter: @CorkUP

Editorial note:

An imprint of Cork University Press.

Blackhall Publishing

www.blackhallpublishing.com

———————————

———————————

What do they publish?

Law

Contact details:

Post: Lonsdale House, Avoca Avenue, Blackrock,
Co. Dublin
Email: info@blackhallpublishing.com
Tel: 00 353 (0)1 278 5090
Twitter: @Blackhall_Pub

Editorial note:

Lonsdale Law is a sister imprint of Blackhall Publishing.

Blackstaff Press

www.blackstaffpress.com

A member of Publishing Ireland,
the Irish Book Publishers' Association

What do they publish?

General non-fiction
History
Fiction

Contact details:

Post: Colourpoint House, Jubilee Business Park,
21 Jubilee Road, Newtownards, BT23 4YH
Email: info@blackstaffpress.com
Tel: 00 44 (0)28 9182 6339
Twitter: @BlackstaffNI

Editorial note:

Acquired by Colourpoint Creative in 2017. Submissions
by post only. Previously self-published works considered.
Patsy Horton, Managing Editor, past President of Publishing
Ireland.

Brandon

www.obrien.ie

———————

A member of Publishing Ireland,
the Irish Book Publishers' Association

———————

What do they publish?

General non-fiction
Literary fiction & crime fiction
Biography

Contact details:

Post: 12 Terenure Road East, Rathgar,
Dublin 6, D06 HD27
Email: books@obrien.ie
Tel: 00 353 (0)1 492 3333
Twitter: @OBrienPress

Editorial note:

Authors include Alice Taylor (*To School through the Fields*)
and Frank McGuinness. Originally founded by Steve
McDonogh, Brandon acquired by O'Brien Press in 2011.

Carysfort Press

www.carysfortpress.com

———————

———————

What do they publish?

Drama
Music
Humanities

Contact details:

Post: 58 Woodfield, Scholarstown Road,
Rahtfarnham, Dublin 16
Email: info@carysfortpress.com
Tel: 00 353 (1) 493 7383
Twitter: n/a

Editorial note:

Founded in 1998, particularly well-known for Theatre
Studies.

Chartered Accountants Ireland

www.charteredaccountants.ie

———————

A member of Publishing Ireland,
the Irish Book Publishers' Association

———————

What do they publish?

Accountancy
Taxation
Management

Contact details:

Post: Chartered Accountants House,
47-49 Pearse St, Dublin 2
Email: michael.diviney@charteredaccountants.ie
Tel: 00 353 (1) 637 7200
Twitter: @CharteredAccIrl

Editorial note:

Michael Diviney, Director of Publishing, is a 2017 board
member of Publishing Ireland.

Church of Ireland Publishing

www.cip.ireland.anglican.org

A member of Publishing Ireland,
the Irish Book Publishers' Association

What do they publish?

Church of Ireland related projects

Contact details:

Post: The Representive Church Body Library,
Braemor Park, Churchtown, Dublin 14
Email: susan.hood@rcbdub.org
Tel: 00 353 (1) 492 3979
Twitter: n/a

Editorial note:

Authors required to cover publication costs.

Clarus Press

www.claruspress.ie

A member of Publishing Ireland,
the Irish Book Publishers' Association

What do they publish?

Irish law

Contact details:

Post: Griffith Campus, South Circular Road, Dublin 2
Email: davidmccartney@claruspress.ie
Tel: 00 353 (1) 415 0439
Twitter: @ClarusPress

Editorial note:

Also publish the *Dublin University Law Journal* and
Irish Business Law Review.

Cló Iar-Chonnacht

www.cic.ie

––––––––––

A member of Publishing Ireland,
the Irish Book Publishers' Association

––––––––––

What do they publish?

Irish language fiction
Irish language non-fiction
Irish language children's
Irish language poetry

Contact details:

Post: Sailearna Business Park, Inverin, Co Galway
Email: eolas@cic.ie
Tel: 00 353 (0)91 593 307
Twitter: @ClolarChonnacht

Editorial note:

Founded in 1985 by Micheál Ó Conghaile.

Cois Life

www.coislife.ie

A member of Publishing Ireland,
the Irish Book Publishers' Association

What do they publish?

Irish language fiction
Irish language academic
Irish language children's
Irish language poetry & drama

Contact details:

Post: 204 DMG House, Deansgrange Business Park,
Deansgrange, Co. Dublin, A94 A4A6
Email: eolas@coislife.ie
Tel: 00 353 (0)1 219 0223
Twitter: @CoisLife

Editorial note:

Founded in 1995, currently publishing between
6 and 8 titles per year.

Collins Press

www.collinspress.ie

A member of Publishing Ireland,
the Irish Book Publishers' Association

What do they publish?

General non-fiction
History
Sport
Walking guides

Contact details:

Post: West Link Park, Doughcloyne, Wilton,
Cork, Co. Cork
Email: submissions@collinspress.ie
Tel: 00 353 (0)21 4347717
Twitter: @CollinsPress

Editorial note:

Founded in 1989, one of Ireland's best-known publishers.
Submissions accepted by post and email.

Cottage Publications

www.cottage-publications.com

What do they publish?

General non-fiction
Local history

Contact details:

Post: 15 Ballyhay Road, Donaghadee, Co. Down,
Northern Ireland, BT21 0NG.
Email: info@cottage-publications.com
Tel: 00 44 (0)28 9188 8033
Twitter: @CottagePubs

Editorial note:

Publications include *Bangor in the Seventies* and *Just for
the Thrill: Competitive Motorcycling in
Ulster in the Seventies.*

Colourpoint Creative

www.colourpointbooks.co.uk

A member of Publishing Ireland,
the Irish Book Publishers' Association

What do they publish?

General non-fiction
Local history
Transport

Contact details:

Post: Colourpoint House, Jubilee Business Park,
21 Jubilee Road, Newtownards, Northern Ireland,
BT23 4YH
Email: info@colourpoint.co.uk
Tel: 0044 (0) 48 9182 6339
Twitter: @colourpoint

Editorial note:

Acquired Blackstaff Press in 2017. Queries by email but
submissions by post.

The Columba Press

www.columba.ie

_____

A member of Publishing Ireland,
the Irish Book Publishers' Association

_____

What do they publish?

Religion
Spirituality

Contact details:

Post: 23 Merrion Square North, Dublin 2
Email: garry@columba.ie
Tel: 00 353 (0)1 687 4096
Twitter: @ColumbaPress

Editorial note:

Published _The Opal and The Pearl_, bestseller spring 2017.
Also run Currach Books.

Cork University Press

www.corkuniversitypress.com

A member of Publishing Ireland,
the Irish Book Publishers' Association

What do they publish?

Academic
Humanities
History
Sport

Contact details:

Post: Youngline Industrial Estate,
Pouladuff Road, Cork
Email: corkuniversitypress@ucc.ie
Tel: 00 353 (0) 21 490 2980
Twitter: @CorkUP

Editorial note:

Published *Atlas of the Great Irish Famine* and *Secrets of the
Irish Landscape*. Also run Attic Press and
Atrium Press.

Currach Press

www.currach.ie

———————

A member of Publishing Ireland,
the Irish Book Publishers' Association

———————

What do they publish?

General non-fiction
Fiction
Poetry
Photography

Contact details:

Post: 23 Merrion Square North, Dublin 2
Email: garry@columba.ie
Tel: 00 353 (0)1 687 4096
Twitter: @CurrachPress

Editorial note:

The general imprint of Columba Press. Recent publications
include *Best Loved Poems: Favourite Poems from the
South of Ireland.*

Dalkey Archive Press

www.dalkeyarchive.com

––––––––––

A member of Publishing Ireland,
the Irish Book Publishers' Association

––––––––––

What do they publish?

Literary fiction

Contact details:

Post: Centre for Literary & Translation Studies, Trinity
College, 36 Fenian Street, Dublin 2
Email: contact@dalkeyarchive.com
Tel: 001 361 485 4563 (USA)
Twitter: @Dalkey_Archive

Editorial note:

Publisher of Eileen Battersby's *Teethmarks on my Tongue*.

Dedalus Press

www.dedaluspresss.com

———————

———————

What do they publish?

Poetry

Contact details:

Post: 13 Moyclare Road, Baldoyle, Dublin 13
Email: editor@dedaluspress.com
Tel: 00 353 (0)1 839 2034
Twitter: @dedaluspress

Editorial note:

Founded in 1985 by John F. Deane, recent publications
include *If Ever you Go: A Map of Dublin in Poetry & Song.*

Doire Press

www.doirepress.com

———————

———————

What do they publish?

Poetry
Literary fiction
Drama

Contact details:

Post: Aille, Inverin, County Galway
Email: doirepress@gmail.com
Tel: 00 353 (0)91 593290
Twitter: @Doirepress

Editorial note:

Authors include Kevin Barry, Mike McCormack, Mary
Costello. Books shortlisted for the Forward Prize 2013 and
won the Shine/Strong Award 2016.

Doubleday Ireland

www.transworldireland.ie

A member of Publishing Ireland,
the Irish Book Publishers' Association

What do they publish?

General non-fiction
Literary fiction

Contact details:

Post: Suites 47-51, Morrison Chambers, 32 Nassau
Street, Dublin 2
Email: info@transworldireland.ie
Tel: 00 353 (0) 1 775 8683
Twitter: @PenguinRandomIE

Editorial note:

Part of Penguin Random House Group. Authors
include Donal Ryan (*The Spinning Heart*) and Hilary
Fannin (*Hopscotch*). Unsolicited submissions accepted.
Submissions by email only.

Flyleaf Press

www.ancestornetwork.ie/flyleaf

———————

———————

What do they publish?

Genealogy

Contact details:

Post: 4 Spencer Villas, Glenageary, Co. Dublin
Email: books@flyleaf.ie
Tel: 00 353 (0)1 285 4658
Twitter: @flyleafpress

Editorial note:

Became the publishing arm of Ancestor Network
in 2014.

Four Courts Press

www.fourcourtspress.ie

———————

———————

What do they publish?

Academic
History
Medieval studies

Contact details:

Post: 7 Malpas Street, Dublin, D08 YD81
Email: info@fourcourtspress.ie
Tel: 00 353 (0)1 453 4668
Twitter: @FourCourtsPress

Editorial note:

Founded in 1970 by Michael Adams (1937–2009), who was
awarded an honorary doctorate by TCD in 2005 for services
to academic life.

The Gallery Press

www.gallerypress.com

———————

A member of Publishing Ireland,
the Irish Book Publishers' Association

———————

What do they publish?

Poetry
Drama

Contact details:

Post: Loughcrew, Oldcastle, Co Meath
Email: n/a
Tel: 00 353 (0)49 8541779
Twitter: @TheGalleryPress

Editorial note:

Authors include Brian Friel, Paul Muldoon, Derek Mahon.
Submissions by post only.

Gill Books

www.gill.ie

A member of Publishing Ireland,
the Irish Book Publishers' Association

What do they publish?

Lifestyle
General non-fiction
Children's
Current affairs
History

Contact details:

Post: Hume Avenue, Park West, Dublin, D12 YV96
Email: dmarsh@gill.ie
Tel: 00 353 (0)1 500 9500
Twitter: @Gill_Books

Editorial note:

Formerly Gill & Macmillan, Ireland's largest indigenous
publisher. Also run Gill Education and Gill Distribution.

Glasnevin Publishing

www.glasnevinpublishing.com

A member of Publishing Ireland,
the Irish Book Publishers' Association

What do they publish?

Academic
Technical

Contact details:

Post: 13 Upper Baggot Street, 2nd Floor, Dublin 4
Email: info@glasnevinpublishing.com
Tel: n/a
Twitter: @GlasnevinPublis

Editorial note:

Established in 2007.

An Gúm

www.forasnagaeilge.ie

A member of Publishing Ireland,
the Irish Book Publishers' Association

What do they publish?

Irish language children's fiction
Irish language children's non-fiction

Contact details:

Post: 7 Merrion Square, Dublin 2
Email: angum@forasnagaeilge.ie
Tel: 00 353 (0)1 889 2800
Twitter: n/a

Editorial note:

An Gúm is part of Foras na Gaeilge.
Also well-known for educational books.

Hachette Books Ireland

www.hachettebooksireland.ie

———————

A member of Publishing Ireland,
the Irish Book Publishers' Association

———————

What do they publish?

Literary fiction
Crime fiction
General non-fiction
Sport
Lifestyle

Contact details:

Post: 8 Castlecourt Centre, Castleknock, Dublin 15
Email: submissions@hbgi.ie
Tel: 00 353 (0)1 824 6288
Twitter: @HachetteIre

Editorial note:

Irish division of the Hachette Book Group. Email
submissions only. Fiction titles must be agented.
Unsolicited submissions for non-fiction are accepted.

The History Press Ireland

www.thehistorypress.ie

———————

A member of Publishing Ireland,
the Irish Book Publishers' Association

———————

What do they publish?

History
General non-fiction & current affairs
Photography
Local history

Contact details:

Post: 50 City Quay, Dublin 2
Email: info@thehistorypress.ie
Tel: 00 353 (0)1 244 9470
Twitter: @THP_Ireland

Editorial note:

Award-winning Irish division of The History Press Group.
Authors include President Mary McAleese, Michael
Nicholson, Ronan McGreevy. Publishing Director, Ronan
Colgan, 2017 President of Publishing Ireland.

Irish Academic Press

www.irishacademicpress.ie

———————

A member of Publishing Ireland,
the Irish Book Publishers' Association

———————

What do they publish?

Academic
History
Biography

Contact details:

Post: Tuckmill House, 10 George's Street,
Newbridge, Co Kildare
Email: conor.graham@iap.ie
Tel: 00 353 (0)45 432 497
Twitter: @IAP_MERRION

Editorial note:

Irish Academic Press is the academic imprint of Merrion
Press. Conor Graham is a 2017 board member of
Publishing Ireland.

The Irish Manuscripts Commission

www.irishmanuscripts.ie

A member of Publishing Ireland,
the Irish Book Publishers' Association

What do they publish?

Collections and republications of
academic source material

Contact details:

Post: 45 Merrion Square, Dublin 2
Email: publishingproposals@irishmanuscripts.ie
Tel: 00 353 (0)1 676 1610
Twitter: @irishmanuscripts

Editorial note:

Founded in 1928, aims to preserve primary source material
for academics, primarily in the field of Irish Studies.

Leabhar Breac

www.leabharbreac.com

What do they publish?

Irish language fiction
Irish language non-fiction
Irish language children's

Contact details:

Post: Indreabhán, Co na Gallimhe
Email: eolas@breacan.ie
Tel: 00 353 (0)91 593 592
Twitter: @BreacEolas

Editorial note:

Authors include Cathal Ó Searcaigh. Also publish Irish
language editions of Enid Blyton and George R.R. Martin.

Liberties Press

www.libertiespress.com

What do they publish?

Fiction
Non-fiction
Erotica

Contact details:

Post: n/a
Email: sean@libertiespress.com
Tel: 00 353 (0)86 853 8793
Twitter: @LibertiesPress

Editorial note:

Publishers of *Grange Abbey* (David Delaney) and *Numb*
(Louis La Roc). Publisher is Seán O'Keeffe.

Liffey Press

www.theliffeypress.com

———————

A member of Publishing Ireland,
the Irish Book Publishers' Association

———————

What do they publish?

General non-fiction
Biography
Short stories

Contact details:

Post: 'Clareville', 307 Clontarf Road, Dublin, D03 P046
Email: dgivens@theliffeypress.com
Tel: 00 353 (0)1 8337814
Twitter: n/a

Editorial note:

Submissions by post or email. Publisher is David Givens.

Lilliput Press

www.lilliputpress.ie

A member of Publishing Ireland,
the Irish Book Publishers' Association

What do they publish?

General non-fiction
Literary fiction
History
Biography

Contact details:

Post: 62-63 Sitric Road, Arbour Hill, Dublin 7
Email: editorial@lilliputpress.ie
Tel: 00 353 (0)1 671 1647
Twitter: @LilliputPress

Editorial note:

Authors include Donal Ryan (*The Spinning Heart*) and
special editions of James Joyce and J.P. Donleavy.
Submissions by post only.

Little Island

www.littleisland.ie

———————

A member of Publishing Ireland,
the Irish Book Publishers' Association

———————

What do they publish?

Children's
YA fiction

Contact details:

Post: 7 Kenilworth Park, Dublin 6W
Email: grainne.clear@littleisland.ie
Tel: 00 353 (0)85 2283 060
Twitter: @LittleIslandBks

Editorial note:

Comprehensive submission guidelines on website.
No rhyming picture books. No proposals with 'Snot' in the
title. Multi-award winning publisher.

Lonsdale Law

www.lonsdalelawpublishing.com

What do they publish?

Irish law

Contact details:

Post: Lonsdale House, Avoca Avenue, Blackrock,
Co. Dublin
Email: info@lonsdalelawpublishing.com
Tel: 00 353 (0)1 278 5090
Twitter: @Blackhall_Pub

Editorial note:

The Irish law imprint of Blackhall Publishing.

Maverick House

www.maverickhouse.com

––––––––––

A member of Publishing Ireland,
the Irish Book Publishers' Association

––––––––––

What do they publish?

Current affairs
Non-fiction
True crime

Contact details:

Post: Maverick House, 47 Harrington Street, Dublin 8
Email: info@maverickhouse.com
Tel: 00 353 (0)1 444 6976
Twitter: @Maverick_House

Editorial note:

Strong international focus, particularly on Thailand.
Publisher of *The Siege at Jadotville* (Declan Power),
licensed by Netflix.

Mercier Press

www.mercierpress.ie

A member of Publishing Ireland,
the Irish Book Publishers' Association

What do they publish?

History & biography
Lifestyle
Children's
Adult & YA fiction

Contact details:

Post: Unit 3b Oak House, Bessboro Rd, Blackrock,
Cork, T12 D6CH
Email: commissioning@mercierpress.ie
Tel: 00 353 (0)21 461 4700
Twitter: @IrishPublisher

Editorial note:

Founded in 1944, books include *It's a Long Way from Penny Apples* (Bill Cullen). Email submissions only. Fiction submissions re-opened 2017.

Merrion Press

www.merrionpress.ie

———————

A member of Publishing Ireland,
the Irish Book Publishers' Association

———————

What do they publish?

General non-fiction
History
Biography
Current affairs

Contact details:

Post: Tuckmill House, 10 George's Street,
Newbridge, Co Kildare
Email: conor.graham@iap.ie
Tel: 00 353 (0)45 432 497
Twitter: @IAP_MERRION

Editorial note:

Merrion Press is the general imprint of
Irish Academic Press. Conor Graham is a board member of
Publishing Ireland.

Messenger Publications

www.messenger.ie

———————

A member of Publishing Ireland,
the Irish Book Publishers' Association

———————

What do they publish?

Spirituality
Religion
Jesuit-focussed history

Contact details:

Post: 37 Leeson Street Lower, Dublin 2
Email:info@messenger.ie
Tel: 00 353 (0)1 676 7491
Twitter: n/a

Editorial note:

The publishing house of the Jesuits in Ireland. Publisher
Cecilia West is a board member of Publishing Ireland.

New Binary Press

www.newbinarypress.com

A member of Publishing Ireland,
the Irish Book Publishers' Association

What do they publish?

Poetry
Short fiction
Literary fiction

Contact details:

Post: n/a
Email: info@newbinarypress.com
Tel: n/a
Twitter: @NewBinaryPress

Editorial note:

Cork-based publisher. Submissions by online form, not
email. Also publish literary journal *The Weary Blues*.

New Island

www.newisland.ie

_____

A member of Publishing Ireland,
the Irish Book Publishers' Association

_____

What do they publish?

General non-fiction
Literary fiction
Short story collections
Poetry
Drama

Contact details:

Post: 16 Priory Office Park, Stillorgan, Co Dublin
Email: editor@newisland.ie
Tel: 00 353 (0)1 278 4225
Twitter: @NewIslandBooks

Editorial note:

Winner of BGE 2016 Irish-Published Book of the Year.
Recently partnered with Head of Zeus for the
UK market.

O'Brien Press

www.obrien.ie

———————

A member of Publishing Ireland,
the Irish Book Publishers' Association

———————

What do they publish?

Children's
General non-fiction
History & sport
Gift

Contact details:

Post: 12 Terenure Road East, Rathgar,
Dublin 6, D06 HD27
Email: books@obrien.ie
Tel: 00 353 (0)1 492 3333
Twitter: @OBrienPress

Editorial note:

Award-winning publisher. Acquired Brandon imprint in
2011. Ivan O'Brien 2017 Vice President of
Publishing Ireland.

Oak Tree Press

www.oaktreepress.eu

A member of Publishing Ireland,
the Irish Book Publishers' Association

What do they publish?

Business & management
Human Resources
Marketing

Contact details:

Post: 33 Rochestown Rise, Rochestown, Cork
Email: info@oaktreepress.com
Tel: 00 353 (0)86 244 1633
Twitter: @brianokane

Editorial note:

Publisher is Brian O'Kane.

Orpen Press

www.orpenpress.com

————————

————————

What do they publish?

General non-fiction
Business
Lifestyle

Contact details:

Post: Top Floor, Unit K9, Grants Road, Greenogue
Business Park, Rathcoole, Dublin
Email: gerryk@orpenpress.com
Tel: 00 353 (0)1 401 8855
Twitter: @OrpenPress

Editorial note:

Email submissions preferred.

Penguin Ireland

www.penguinrandomhouse.co.uk

A member of Publishing Ireland,
the Irish Book Publishers' Association

What do they publish?

General non-fiction & current affairs
Fiction
Sport

Contact details:

Post: Suites 47-51, Morrison Chambers,
32 Nassau Street, Dublin 2
Email: submissions@penguinrandomhouse.ie
Tel: 00 353 (0)1 661 7695
Twitter: @PenguinRandomIE

Editorial note:

Irish division of Penguin Random House, world's largest
trade publisher. Includes Penguin Ireland, Doubleday
Ireland, Transworld Ireland. Unsolicited manuscripts
accepted, email preferred.

Peter Lang Ireland

www.peterlang.com

———————

———————

What do they publish?

Academic
Irish studies
Humanities

Contact details:

Post: c/o 52 St Giles, Oxford, OX1 3LU, UK
Email: c.scaife@peterlang.com
Tel: 00 44 (0)1865 514 160
Twitter: @PeterLangOxford

Editorial note:

Irish division of Peter Lang Oxford,
part of the Peter Lang Group.

Poolbeg

www.poolbeg.com

————————

————————

What do they publish?

General non-fiction
Historical fiction
Romance
Children's

Contact details:

Post: Unit 123, Grange Hill,
Baldoyle Industrial Estate, Dublin 13
Email: info@poolbeg.com
Tel: 00 353 (0)1 832 1477
Twitter: @PoolbegBooks

Editorial note:

Includes the Ward River Press imprint for literary fiction.

Roads Publishing

www.roads.co

––––––––––

A member of Publishing Ireland,
the Irish Book Publishers' Association

––––––––––

What do they publish?

Art
Design & fashion
Cultural guides
Roads Classics

Contact details:

Post: Guinness Enterprise Centre,
Taylor's Lane, Dublin 8
Email: publishing@roads.co
Tel: n/a
Twitter: @ROADSpublishing

Editorial note:

Considered Guides series recently launched.
Strong design and production reputation. Maeve Convery a
board member of Publishing Ireland.

Royal Irish Academy

www.ria.ie

A member of Publishing Ireland,
the Irish Book Publishers' Association

What do they publish?

Academic
History
Science
Humanities

Contact details:

Post: 19 Dawson Street, Dublin 2, D02 HH58
Email: R.Hegarty@ria.ie
Tel: 00 353 (0)1 676 2570
Twitter: @RIAdawson

Editorial note:

Publisher of *Judging Dev, Ireland in 100 Objects*. Winner
of BGE Irish-Published Book of the Year 2013. Ruth Hegarty
former President of Publishing Ireland.

Somerville Press

www.somervillepress.com

———————

———————

What do they publish?

General non-fiction
Fiction

Contact details:

Post: Dromore, Bantry, Co. Cork
Email: somervillepress@eircom.net
Tel: 00 353 (0)28 32873
Twitter: n/a

Editorial note:

Fiction includes *The Rule of War* (Aoife Feeney). Non-fiction includes Desmond Fennell's autobiography *About Being Normal*.

The Stinging Fly Press

www.stingingfly.org

———————

A member of Publishing Ireland,
the Irish Book Publishers' Association

———————

What do they publish?

Literary fiction
Short stories

Contact details:

Post: PO Box 6016, Dublin 1
Email: submissions.stingingfly@gmail.com
Tel: n/a
Twitter: @stingingfly

Editorial note:

Book publishing imprint of *The Stinging Fly* literary journal.
Authors include Kevin Barry, Mary Costello, Colin Barrett.
Publisher is Declan Meade.

Swan River Press

www.swanriverpress.ie

———————

———————

What do they publish?

Gothic fiction

Contact details:

Post: n/a
Email: brian@swanriverpress.ie
Tel: n/a
Twitter: @SwanRiverPress

Editorial note:

Submissions by invitation only.

Tirgearr Publishing

www.tirgearrpublishing.com

What do they publish?

Adult fiction
Romance
Erotica

Contact details:

Post: Bethany House, Tower Cross, Mornington
Manor, Co. Meath
Email: info@tirgearrpublishing.com
Tel: n/a
Twitter: @Tirgearr

Editorial note:

Digital publisher, strict formatting guidelines for
submissions.

Tramp Press

www.trampress.com

————————

————————

What do they publish?

Literary fiction

Contact details:

Post: n/a
Email: submissions@tramppress.com
Tel: n/a
Twitter: @TrampPress

Editorial note:

Author awards include The Guardian First Book Award,
BGE Newcomer of the Year, Goldsmiths Prize, Costa
shortlist. Authors include Mike McCormack and
Sara Baume.

Transworld Ireland

www.transworldireland.ie

———————

A member of Publishing Ireland,
the Irish Book Publishers' Association

———————

What do they publish?

General non-fiction
Literary fiction
Sport

Contact details:

Post: Suites 47-51, Morrison Chambers, 32 Nassau
Street, Dublin 2
Email: info@transworldireland.ie
Tel: 00 353 (0)1 775 8683
Twitter: @PenguinRandomIE

Editorial note:

Part of Penguin Random House Group. Authors include
Donal Ryan, Stephen Ferris, Colm O'Regan and Ronan
O'Gara. Awards include BGE Sports Book of the Year, BGE
Newcomer of the Year and Man Booker longlist.

UCD Press

www.ucdpress.ie

A member of Publishing Ireland,
the Irish Book Publishers' Association

What do they publish?

Academic
General non-fiction
History
Lliterary studies

Contact details:

Post: UCD Humanities Institute, Room H103,
Belfield, Dublin 4
Email: ucdpress@ucd.ie
Tel: 00 353 (0)1 716 4680
Twitter: @UCDPress

Editorial note:

Publications include *The Encyclopaedia of Music in Ireland*
and *The Real People of Joyce's Ulysses*. Executive Editor is
Noelle Moran.

Veritas Publications

www.veritasbooksonline.com

A member of Publishing Ireland,
the Irish Book Publishers' Association

What do they publish?

Theology
Spirituality
Philosophy

Contact details:

Post: 7-8 Lower Abbey Street, Dublin 1
Email: donna.doherty@veritas.ie
Tel: 00 353 (0)1 878 8177
Twitter: @VeritasIreland

Editorial note:

Also run the Veritas book retail chain. Publishing
division founded in 1969.

Wordwell Books

www.wordwellbooks.com

A member of Publishing Ireland,
the Irish Book Publishers' Association

What do they publish?

History
Archaeology
Architecture

Contact details:

Post: Unit 9, 78 Furze Road, Sandyford, Dublin 18
Email: nick@wordwellbooks.com
Tel: 00 353 (0)1 293 3568
Twitter: @wordwellbooks

Editorial note:

Also publish the magazines *Books Ireland*, *History Ireland* and *Archaeology Ireland*. Una McConville is a board member of Publishing Ireland.

The Self-Publishers

Carrowmore
www.carrowmore.ie

Post: 50 City Quay, Dublin 2
Email: info@carrowmore.ie
Tel: 00 353 (0)86 600 2951
Twitter: @carrowmore101

Editorial Note:

Carrowmore provides professional editorial, design, print, ebook and publishing services to authors. The company's background is in traditional publishing, with staff working on award-winning books for the general trade.

The idea behind Carrowmore is to give authors access to the same level of professional publishing resources used by traditional publishers, and to provide advice and guidance throughout each project.

All rights are 100% owned by the authors, and 100% of revenue and royalties from sales through the trade and online, including both Amazon and Amazon Kindle sales, go directly to authors.

Genres published include: contemporary fiction, general non-fiction, history, business, children's, poetry.

Carrowmore's Advisory Publishing Director is Ronan Colgan, President of Publishing Ireland, the Irish Book Publishers' Association, and Publishing Director of The History Press Ireland.

Orla Kelly Publishing
www.orlakellypublishing.com

Post: n/a
Tel: n/a
Email: orla@orlakellypublishing.com
Twitter: n/a
Editorial note: bronze, silver and gold packages offered.

Selfpublishbooks.ie
www.selfpublishbooks.ie

Post: Springhill House, Carrigtwohill, Co. Cork
Tel: 00 353 (0)21 488 3370
Email: info@selfpublishbooks.ie
Twitter: @lettertec
Editorial note: the self-publishing arm of Lettertec Print, based in Cork.

Choice Publishing
www.choicepublishing.ie

Post: Barlow House, Narrow West Street, Drogheda, Co. Louth
Tel: 00 353 (0)41 984 1551
Email: info@choicepublishing.ie
Twitter: @choicepublish1
Editorial note: founded by Deirdre Devine and Michelle Bradley.

Red Hen Publishing
www.redhenpublishing.ie

Post: Duagh, Listowel, Co. Kerry
Tel: 00 353 (0)1 68 45942
Email: redhen1@eircom.net
Twitter: n/a
Editorial note: Red Hen Publishing is run by Bridget McAuliffe.

Eprint.ie
www.eprint.ie

Post: 35 Coolmine Industrial Estate,
Blanchardstown, Dublin 15
Tel: 00 353 (0)1 827 8860
Email: contact form on website
Twitter: @eprintbooks
Editorial note: the self-publishing arm of eprint.ie printers.

The Literary Agents

Marianne Gunn O'Connor

Post: Suite 17, Morrison Chambers,
32 Nassau Street, Dublin 2
Email: mgoclitagency@eircom.net
Tel: 00 353 (0)1 677 9100

The Lisa Richards Agency

www.lisarichards.ie
Post: 108 Upper Leeson Street, Dublin 4
Email: faith@lisarichards.ie
Tel: 00 353 (0)1 637 5000

Jonathan Williams Literary Agency

Post: Rosney Mews, Upper Glenageary
Road, Glenageary, Co Dublin
Email: n/a
Tel: 00 353 (0)1 280 3482

The Feldstein Agency

www.thefeldsteinagency.co.uk
Post: 54 Abbey Street, Bangor, BT20 4JB,
Northern Ireland
Email: paul@thefeldsteinagency.co.uk
Tel: 0044 (0)28 9147 2823

Inkwell Writers
www.inkwellwriters.ie
Post: n/a
Email: vanessa@writing.ie
Tel: n/a
Note: run by Vanessa O'Loughlin, founder of
www.writing.ie.

The Book Bureau
Post: Geraldine Nichol, 7 Duncairn Avenue,
Bray, Co. Wicklow
Email: thebookbureau@oceanfree.net
Tel: 00 353 (0)1 276 4996

Author Rights Agency
www.authorrightsagency.com
Post: Svetlana Pironko, 20 Victoria Road,
Rathgar, Dublin 6
Email: submissions@authorrightsagency.com
Tel: n/a
Note: currently closed to unsolicited submissions.

MMB Creative
www.mmbcreative.com
Post: Sallyanne Sweeney, The Old Truman Brewery,
91 Brick Lane, London, E1 6QL, UK
Email: Sallyanne@mmbcreative.com
Note: submission form on website. UK-based, but
strong focus on Irish writing.

The Literary Journals

The Stinging Fly
www.stingingfly.org
@stingingfly

The Dublin Review
www.thedublinreview.com
@TheDublinReview

The Tangerine
www.thetangerinemagazine.com
@thetangerinemag

Gorse
www.gorse.ie
@gorse_journal

Guts
www.thisisguts.com
@Guts_Magazine

Banshee
www.bansheelit.com
@bansheelit

Winter Papers
www.winterpapers.com
@Winterpapers

Irish Pages
www.irishpages.org
@irishpages

The Moth
www.themothmagazine.com
@themothmagazine

Crannóg
www.crannogmagazine.com
@CrannogMag

The SHOp
www.theshop-poetry-magazine.ie
@theSHOpmag

Southword
www.munsterlit.ie
@MunLitCentre

New Dublin Press
www.newdublinpress.org
@NewDublinPress

Cyphers
www.cyphers.ie

Boyne Berries
www.boyneberries.blogspot.ie
@BoyneBerries

Silver Streams
www.silverstreamsjournal.com
@SilverStreamsJL

The Penny Dreadful
www.thepennydreadful.org
@DreadfulP

North West Words
www.northwestwords.com
@_northwestwords

The Bohemyth
www.thebohemyth.com
@TheBohemyth

Icarus
www.icarusmagazine.com
@IcarusTCD

The Scum Gentry
www.the-scum-gentry-alternative-arts.com
@ScumGentryArts

Roadside Fiction
www.roadsidefiction.com
@RoadsideFiction

The Weary Blues
www.thewearyblues.org
@NewBinaryPress

Author Resources

Words Ireland
www.wordsireland.ie
Email: info@wordsireland.ie
Twitter: @WordsIreland

Publishing Ireland
www.publishingireland.com
Email: info@publishingireland.com
Twitter: @PublishingIRL

Children's Books Ireland
www.childrensbooksireland.ie
Email: info@childrensbooksireland.ie
Twitter: @KidsBooksIrel

Poetry Ireland
www.poetryireland.ie
Email: info@poetryireland.ie
Twitter: @poetryireland

Writing.ie
www.writing.ie
Email: vanessa@writing.ie
Twitter: @writing_ie

Irish Writers Union
www.irishwritersunion.org
Email: info@irishwritersunion.org
Twitter: @WritersUnion_ie

Irish Writers Centre
www.irishwriterscentre.ie
Email: info@writerscentre.ie
Twitter: @IrishWritersCtr

Literature Ireland
www.literatureireland.com
Email: info@literatureireland.com
Twitter: @LitIreland

Munster Literature Centre
www.munsterlit.ie
Email: munsterlit@eircom.net
Twitter: @MunLitCentre

The Arts Council
www.artscouncil.ie
Email: aoife.moynihan@artscouncil.ie
Twitter: @artscouncil_ie